ABOVE SAN FRANCISCO

by
ROBERT CAMERON

*A New Collection of Historical and
Original Aerial Photographs*

*with text by
ARTHUR HOPPE*

CAMERON and COMPANY   SAN FRANCISCO, CALIFORNIA

Fireworks emblazon the sky to celebrate the 50th anniversaries of the city's two great bridges. On the right is the Bay Bridge, opened in 1936, and on the left the Golden Gate Bridge, which linked Marin to the City just a year later. You can see the lights of the pleasure boats that dotted the Bay for a close-up look at the pyrotechnics.

Herb Caen's Baghdad-by-the-Bay, carved from some fragile alabaster, basks for a magical moment under a cloud-puffed sky.

(opposite) From high above the East Bay, the salt flats carve an abstract art work worthy of a Thiebaud or a Diebenkorn.

TABLE OF CONTENTS

Such a book as this does not reach publication without more than the usual cooperation
from many people. So, for their encouragement and expertise, I thank the following:

Patricia Akre, Hatsuro Aizawa, Anthony Cameron, Todd Cameron, Madelaine Cassidy, Paolo Cornacchia,
Jeffreys Corner, Tracy Davis, Gary Fong, John Goy, David Gregory, Gladys Hansen, Linda Henry,
Tina Hodge, Gloria Hoppe, Gladys Horiuchi, Ed Mein, Ed Moose, Patricia O'Grady,
Mary Petrin-Kehoe, Noboru Watanabe, Al Wilsey, Frederick Zieber.

For special research and expert helicoptering, Teri McClelland and John McClelland.
Additional piloting:
David Duffin, Andrew Kleinberg, Bruce McLean, Sandy Sauders, Steve Sullivan, Ed Ybarrola.

For assistance in researching the historical aerial photography, acknowledgement is made to:

MARILYN BLAISDELL COLLECTION for page 28: Clyde H. Sunderland, Photographer;
page 44: R.J. Waters, photographer; page 48: Terrell Miller, photographer;
page 50: Worder, photographer; pages 56 and 75: photographers unknown.

SAN FRANCISCO CHRONICLE LIBRARY for page 34: Sponagel-Herrman photographer;
page 38: photographer unknown; page 46: U.S. Army photograph;
page 52: U.S. Army photograph; page 80: photographer unknown.

CALIFORNIA HISTORICAL SOCIETY for page 36: G.E. Russell, photographer;
page 40: Clyde H. Sunderland, photographer.

ED MEIN COLLECTION for page 108.

CAMERON and COMPANY

680 8ᵀᴴ Street, Suite 205 San Francisco, CA. 94103, 415-558-8455 800-779-5582 Fax 415-558-8657
www.abovebooks.com

Library of Congress Catalog Number: 98-93262
ABOVE SAN FRANCISCO ISBN: 0-918684-73-0
©1998 by Robert Cameron and Company, Inc. All rights reserved.

First Printing, 1998
Second Printing, 2000
Third Printing, 2004
Fourth Printing, 2006
Fifth Printing, 2008

Book design by
JANE OLAUG KRISTIANSEN

Color Processing by The New Lab, San Francisco. Cameras by Pentax.
Helicopters by San Francisco Helicopter Tours. Color Xerography by Copy Service, San Francisco.
Typography by Minnowillo, San Francisco.
Printed in China

INTRODUCTION by ARTHUR HOPPE

San Francisco! "The most attractive, most civilized, most desirable city in the country." Holiday magazine rhapsodized more than a quarter of a century ago, "Nobody else's town is quite so beautiful or cosmopolitan or delightfully giddy."

We San Franciscans are accustomed to being slathered with such praise, but it is good to have it confirmed in the lyric photographs by Robert Cameron that follow. The blessings of nature not only define where we live but how we live. Rome has hills, London has fog, Hong Kong has a bay, but here we relish all of these. Unlike those bustling metropolises, the living is easy. We have no snow to shovel, no heat that swelters. The good little restaurant is just down the block, the verdant park is around the corner, the theater, the opera, the symphony are all quite worthy. And in New York or Hartford or Peoria people rarely stop to look at the view.

Our symbol has become that rolling tourist attraction, the cable car, and rightly so. For as they glide along at a stately twelve miles an hour, bells gaily ringing, they set both the city's tone and pace. This is a branch office town. The talented young man in the huge corporation works his way up to become branch manager. "Great news, George," says the head office back east. "We've been watching your work, and the job of assistant associate vice president here in New York (or Hartford or Peoria) is yours. You may well be top dog some day."

The young man with get-up-and-go gets up and is gone. He packs up his reluctant family and heads determinably east to shovel and swelter and get run over by pedestrians because he burns with ambition. Others, however, reject the bitch goddess and remain in this cool, gray city because they love their lives. The New Yorker looks down on us as hopeless losers. We however, prefer to think of ourselves as wise philosophers. They, like the Germans, live to work. We, like the French, work to live.

And we live in an enclave unlike any other. It is a peninsula seven miles square bursting with hills and sweeping vistas. We like to say our little world is bounded on three sides by water and on the fourth by reality. We are rich in both diversity and perversity. When friends from Washington ask with deep frowns what is going on in California politics, I can only shrug and reply, "How do I know? I live in San Francisco."

When the California electorate votes overwhelmingly in favor of such fashionable issues as banning affirmative action or cracking down on illegal aliens, we are alone on the other side of the chasm. The causes that unify us are (1) dividing California in half and (2) making San Francisco an independent city state. We strongly support both impossibilities.

Our independence is in our blood. We are the heirs of adventurous Spanish soldiers, roistering '49ers, tough sea captains and flinty bonanza kings. For more than a century, our population has swelled with Asians who crossed the vast ocean, with pioneers who trudged across the endless plains and by Latinos who climbed the border fences – all of them driven to improve their lives.

Yet now that we've arrived – some of us generations ago – we are no longer in a hurry because we're not going anywhere. We are contented where we are. Easterners have accused us of being smug, and rightly so. We have much to be smug about. We are, the pollsters tells us, "America's favorite city." We are a Mecca for tourists, and they have become our leading industry. They crowd us off our cable cars and take our favorite tables in our restaurants, but we treasure them, for each is silent testimony to the desirability of living where we live.

So we smile at their blue knees when they insist on wearing shorts in the summertime. And when there's a chance, we delight in quoting them a remark wrongly attributed to Mark Twain: "The coldest winter I ever spent was one summer in San Francisco."

But that's hyperbole. It's never really cold here; it's cool. Our cool, rainy winters are succeeded by our cool, foggy summers – an equitable climate, we say. No hurricanes uproot our trees, no tornadoes rip away our roofs, no floods inundate our hills.

But nature is rarely all-forgiving, nor has she exempted San Francisco from her wrath. As the second millennium draws to a close, two monstrous tectonic plates are grinding inexorably beneath this city of hubris toward an inevitable upheaval. My father survived the earthquake of 1906. I have seen two damaging temblors in my lifetime. But this, say the seismologists, will be what the media calls "The Big One."

We seldom think about it. We rarely talk about it. Like the villagers on the slopes of Mt. Etna, we pursue our leisurely lives and shrug at the prospect of disaster. When it hits, we will rebuild our city as we have done before, we confidently say, and resume our halcyon pace.

Yet this unspoken catastrophe to come gives San Francisco an ephemeral air. There is an impermanence to all that's on this uneasy earth over which we so lightly tread. We live, if you will, in another Camelot.

For more than a century, writers and poets have tried desperately to grasp this elusive Camelot. It is, perhaps, more a quest for a photographer. Surely its God-given beauty has never been more thoroughly captured than in these exquisite photographs by Robert Cameron. From his helicopter soaring over this idyllic setting, Bob Cameron has looked down with a God-like eye and recorded with his camera what God sees. He has recorded it for you, gentle reader, and for generations yet to come. Here, in these pages, is proof that, yes, once there was a Camelot.

THE BAY AND BRIDGES

The Golden Gate Bridge plunges out of the fog to attack Fort Baker *(opposite)*. This is one of a series of forts that have been defending the entrance to the Bay since 1850 from an enemy who never came. Today, the Fort is part of the vast park lands known as The Golden Gate National Recreation Area.

The summer fog erupts into a miniature Mount Fujiyama off the Berkeley shore. In the foreground is the eastern portion of the Bay Bridge, damaged in the Loma Prieta earthquake. It is being replaced by a parallel span. *(opposite)* The fog cuddles up to the north tower of the Golden Gate Bridge.

The tide swirls around the south tower of the Golden Gate Bridge as a sailboat beats to windward far below.

The Bay Bridge.

A fish-eye camera puts the Bay Area where it belongs – on top of the world.

(*opposite*) The Golden Gate Bridge.

That ultimate in weapons of war, a nuclear submarine, carrying enough missiles to incinerate a half dozen cities, cruises menacingly through the peaceful waters of San Francisco Bay.

(opposite) How lovely prisons look from the air. This, of course, is Alcatraz, known to a generation of convicts as "The Rock." Serving their hard time in this toughest of all U.S. penitentiaries were Al Capone, Machine Gun Kelly and Robert Stroud, "The Birdman of Alcatraz." Today, it's a national park, teeming with tourists ferried over from San Francisco.

The Richmond San Rafael Bridge stretches across San Pablo Straits at the north end of the Bay like the bones of some broken-backed dinosaur. When it opened in 1956, architect Frank Lloyd Wright singled it out as one of the ugliest bridges ever built.

Two utilitarian bridges span the South Bay. On the top is the San Mateo Bridge, which links the northern Peninsula to Hayward and at the bottom is the Dumbarton, connecting Palo Alto and the Fremont area.

Like a silver butterfly, one of San Francisco's two beloved fire-boats chugs out to greet a new arrival. In addition to welcoming guests, each boat can pump 10,000 gallons a minute into fires on piers and ships.

(opposite) The lovely Queen Elizabeth II glides past Fisherman's Wharf on her only visit to the Bay Area in 1978.

Verdant Angel Island, a refuge for deer, quail and picnickers, rises from the bay. Across Raccoon Strait lies the village of Tiburon and, in the distance, Mt. Tamalpaias. The island served as a detention camp for hostile Arizona Indians in the 1870s and as a Quarantine and Immigration Station until World War II.

(*opposite*) A harbor tour boat etches a sweeping curve away from Pier 39. The four rows of floating docks on which the sea lions live and roar for the tourist trade are just inside the harbor entrance. That's Fishermen's Wharf at the lower left.

Two views of Point Bonita where the lighthouse perched on its pinnacle of rock warns ships approaching the Golden Gate of the ominous rocks below.

These twins arrived 31 years apart. The western span *(foreground)* over the Carquinez Strait was erected in 1927. To accommodate ever-increasing traffic, the eastern bridge was built in 1958. Now engineers are planning to replace the older one in a game of bridge-building leap frog.

(opposite) The late afternoon sun silvers the Golden Gate, and the first wisps of fog blur the valleys of the Marin headlands. That's Mt. Tamalpais in the upper right hand corner.

Here's Treasure Island being born. The 380 acres of landfill were created for the 1939 World's Fair. Afterward it served as a naval base until San Francisco took it over in 1997. The city is still trying to decide what to do with it.

(opposite) Treasure Island today is mostly unused open space. The buildings tell its history: Some date back to the '39 World's Fair and some are Naval barracks left over from World War II.

The candy-striped Mile Rock lighthouse juts up from the sea just a mile from the Golden Gate. Back in the '60s, Bob Cameron landed his helicopter on its flat roof to await the arrival of an incoming battleship.

(opposite) The Golden Gate Bridge points like an arrow to the sprawling green Presidio. Beyond that lie the serried rows of houses of the Richmond and Sunset Districts, divided by Golden Gate Park.

THE CITY

Washington Square in the foreground lies at the center of North Beach, while Coit Tower rises from the crest of Telegraph Hill at the upper right. *(opposite)* The skyscrapers glow in the evening light as the first puffs herald the arrival of the summer fog.

The pace of the city was slower before the bridges were built, but the Bay was busier with all sorts of craft scooting this way and that. *(opposite)* Today, the shipping piers are virtually empty and a single ferryboat docks at the Ferry Building.

The Sunset District crawls up from the Ocean below and huddles against Golden Gate Park at the upper left in this scene from before World War II. The rest is still a barren expanse of sand dunes.

(opposite) Look what Henry Doelger and other builders did: Row upon row of what folk singer Malvina Reynolds called "ticky-tacky boxes." Most are nearly identical "junior fives" with stucco facades, a garage underneath, a tiny patch of lawn out front and maybe a tree in the minimal back yard.

With the rest of the nation throwing up more freeways every day, San Franciscans are happier tearing them down. Here is the double-decker Central Freeway crossing Market Street in 1965 with Twin Peaks in the background.

(opposite) After the Loma Prieta quake, the top deck had to be removed. A fine civic fight arose on whether to tear the rest of it down or widen it into a two-way, single-deck freeway. Thus far, the freeway forces are ahead, but it's a close call.

Sutro Baths, the old swimming hole for generations of San Franciscans. Built in 1896 on the western shore of the city, the baths featured water slides and six huge pools of varying temperatures. In 1937, one leg of an L-shaped pool was converted into an ice rink. The huge structure, ice rink and all, was demolished in a spectacular fire in 1966.

(opposite) Today the baths are but a large hole in the sand dunes. The famed Cliff House restaurant still stands to the right overlooking Seal Rocks.

Downtown San Francisco ca. 1930. No Bay Bridge yet. Ferry slips are
just visible near the Ferry Building. Piers at water's edge are busy.

(opposite) The Ferry Building has been swallowed up by the cluster of new high-
rises in the Financial District. Both the pointy Transamerica Pyramid (top, center)
and the brooding Bank of America behemoth to its right stirred the aesthetic wrath
of many a San Franciscan.

No. 118 - California St. Hill from Merchants Exchange looking West   R.J. Waters & Co.

Looking up California street to Nob Hill after the 1906 Quake. The Fairmont Hotel on the right survived as did towered Grace Cathedral across the street. The Cathedral has since moved a block up the hill behind the hotel.

(opposite) Now we're looking up California street to Nob Hill today. There's Grace Cathedral at the crest. Just below it is the Fairmont Hotel and its adjacent tower. That towering, brown, Godzilla of a structure that dominates the scene belongs to the Bank of America.

(0157-32-1-15) (10-31-27-1P) (12-5000)
SAN FRANCISCO CAL.

The city before World War II. The bridges across the bay are only a dream. Ships dot the piers, and the Russ Building *(center)* rises a towering 31 stories, making it San Francisco's largest and tallest building.

(opposite) Bridges reach out across the Bay to Oakland and Marin. Many of the piers are gone, and, as for the mighty Russ Building, it has disappeared among the skyscrapers that have sprouted up downtown.

Here's the heart of downtown San Francisco as it looked a century ago. The photograph, taken from the top of the old Call Building, shows Union Square on the right before the erection of the Dewey Monument in 1902. Virtually all the buildings around the square were destroyed in the 1906 Quake, but the monument survived.

(*opposite*) Today, the monument pokes its slender finger skyward from the center of the square. In her artistic youth, Alma de Bretteville (Big Alma) Spreckels posed for the figure atop the towering pedestal. She is holding a trident to salute Admiral Dewey for his victory at Manila Bay and a wreath to commemorate the assassinated President McKinley. Big Alma went on to become one of San Francisco's grandest *Grandes Dames*

The lovely odor of chocolate used to emanate from the sprawling Ghirardelli factory on the lower right. *(opposite)* Today, it's an architecturally tasteful mall of shops and restaurants. To its left is the Galileo High School football field and, beyond that, Fort Mason.

A fleet of Flying Fortresses sail over Fort Mason at the end of World War II. The fort was the embarkation point for thousands of servicemen heading for battles in the Pacific. On the right is the Muni Pier, a massive structure built by the WPA. On a good day, you might find several dozen fishermen using it to cast their lines and drop their crab nets.

(*opposite*) Fort Mason today, now a center for the performing arts and cultural events, including the annual San Francisco Blues Festival underway here in the Fort's Great Meadow. Several dozen fishermen are still casting their lines from the Muni Pier.

The afternoon fog mercifully swallows up ungainly Sutro Tower,
thus improving the aesthetic environment.

(opposite) San Francisco and its Bay. The Transamerica Pyramid pokes its pointy finger
skyward at the upper left. No building is so highly admired or so ardently loathed by San
Franciscans. That mammoth box (center left) is the Federal Building, which architectural
critic Alan Temko said should be occupied only by Nazi storm troopers.

We're looking down Geary boulevard toward Market street just before World War II. That's a cemetery to the left of the broad avenue and the Lone Mountain College for Women on the right. The sprawling brick building with the square tower in the foreground is Roosevelt Junior High School, long one of the city's best.

(opposite) The cemetery has vanished to make room for the living, and Lone Mountain is now part of the University of San Francisco. Otherwise little has changed except for the new skyscrapers clustered downtown.

Here is freeway removal's finest hour. In 1968, the double-decked Broadway Freeway and its ramps snaked from the Bay Bridge past the Ferry Building to the financial district and out toward North Beach and Chinatown.

(opposite) After the Loma Prieta quake, it was demolished. A landscaped boulevard and esplanade is taking its place. That's the weekly Farmer's Market displaying its edibles to the left of the Ferry Building.

When the Blue Angels are whizzing this way and that, helicopters are grounded. So Bob Cameron climbed atop the neighboring Bank of America building on a Saturday to take this shot of them streaking past the Transamerica tower. He was accidentally locked out and contemplated 48 hours without food or water. Then he remembered that Monday, too, was a holiday. Fortunately, his calls for help were heard within hours.

(opposite) El Niño stirs the surf to a frothy white blanket at Ocean Beach. That strip of green is Golden Gate Park which divides the Sunset District in the foreground from the Richmond District.

A lone winner approaches the finish line of the annual Bay-to-Breakers Race. Somewhere behind him 70,000 other entrants are running, jogging, walking and dancing from the Ferry Building out past the old Dutch Windmill at the western end of Golden Gate Park.

(opposite) The Hall of Flowers gleams whitely in its sylvan setting in Golden Gate Park. The vast greenhouse, a widely respected conservatory, was damaged in the Loma Prieta Quake and was closed to the public for restoration.

Glowing in the sunset is the California Palace of the Legion of Honor, one of the city's three major art museums. Its triumphal arch and colonnades were modeled after the classic 18th Century Palais de la Legion d'Honeur in Paris. It was dedicated in 1924 to Californians who died in the first World War. In 1985 it underwent a three-year, $37 million renovation.

(opposite) The new Museum of Modern Art *(upper center)* pokes its blind eye skyward over the Moscone Convention Center and Yerba Buena Gardens where a multiplex cinema and other attractions are still under construction. The stepped building at the far left is the new Marriott Hotel, known to San Franciscans as "The Giant Juke Box." "The best view of the city is from the glassed-in lounge at the top," said one critic, "because from there, you can't see the Marriott."

The University of California Medical Center, one of the nation's most respected teaching hospitals, nestles against wooded Sutro Forest. Ugly Sutro Tower raises its spindly girders from the mountaintop to broadcast radio and television far and wide.

At the lower right is the Bayshore Freeway's deadly "Hospital Curve," which has taken many a motorist's life. Rising above it is Potrero Hill, home to writers and artists.

Golfers were infuriated when Alma de Bretteville (Big Alma) Spreckels decided to build her Palace of the Legion of Honor Museum in the center of the Lincoln Park Golf Course. They were placated, however, when Big Alma hired an eminent golf course architect, W. Herbert Fowler, to redesign the fairways.

(opposite) Six of San Francisco's golf courses are clustered near the Beach. The Olympic Club's three courses are in the foreground, although a goodly segment of its nine-hole course clinging to the cliffs collapsed during the 1998 El Niño storms. The others (clockwise) are Harding, San Francisco and the Lake Merced Golf Clubs.

Saints Peter and Paul, all creamy white, looks out over Washington Square, where aging paisanos still sit on the benches smoking their twisted cigars and telling stories of long ago Italy. This is the very heart of North Beach, a Mecca for lovers of pasta and red wine.

The new St. Mary's Cathedral has been hailed by critics as a break-through in modern church archi-tecture. Impious locals, however, refer to it as "the washing-machine agitator."

Temple Emanu-El is the center of the city's Reform Jewish community. Senator Dianne Feinstein's home is the first house backing on the Temple grounds at the upper left.

Grace Cathedral stands atop Nob Hill, its spire pointing heavenward. The cornerstone was laid in 1910, but what with wars and the Depression, it wasn't dedicated until 1964. This is the church for San Francisco's socially prominent, lovers of fine music and admirers of French Gothic architecture.

The pyramidal Transamerica building is seen in its entirety, including its modern colonnade that wraps around the ground floor. Here it looks threatened by that hulking, Darth Varder-like Bank of America building.

(opposite) This is the summit of Pacific Heights, both geographically and monetarily. In the center is the last undeveloped lot, the one-time site of Grant Grammar School, which many a prominent San Franciscan attended. The acre it occupied was recently sold for more than $13 million. To its right is the Gold Coast, the last three blocks of Broadway where the Gettys, the Jewitts and other tycoons have their mansions.

Great plans are underway to convert the officers' homes and barracks in the centuries-old Presidio to private housing for some 1600 families. The sylvan setting overlooking the beach at Crissy Field and the Golden Gate makes it prime real estate.

(opposite) Daredevil Art Smith thrilled the crowd at the 1915 World's Fair with an early version of skywriting which, as the photo shows, was none too legible.

Here the fish-eye camera captures the entire city.

(opposite) San Francisco's architectural pride and joy are its
Victorian houses. Here's a large batch to choose from.

More than 83,000 alumni and other fans jam Stanford Stadium to cheer for Stanford or Cal in this 100th Big Game between the two arch rivals. Stanford won this one, 22-21.

(opposite) The green, rolling Stanford Golf Course with the red tile roofs of the University in the background. Rising from their midst is the Hoover Tower. Today it's a bastion of some of the nation's most formidable conservatively oriented scholars.

It all began in 1927 when San Francisco purchased 1,509 acres on the Bay fifteen miles south of the city from the Mills estate and constructed its first airport, Mills Field. San Franciscans complain that it has been under construction ever since.

By 1947, the name had been changed to the more impressive San Francisco Airport. The new terminal, complete with plaza and fountain, is to the left of the original building.

After thirteen more years of construction, we now had San Francisco International Airport with acres of parking and a lot longer walk to your plane.

Today's airport sprawls over 5,171 acres. More than forty million people a year pass through its gates. Parking is now in a six-story garage. Thanks to progress, passengers changing planes may have as much as a half-mile walk from one gate to another. As you can see on the left, the airport is still undergoing major construction – this time a giant $2.4 billion International Terminal. It will be as huge as all three present terminals combined.

Air Force One lands safely at Moffett Field, a short drive from Stanford University, where the President and Mrs. Clinton will visit their daughter, Chelsea.

The wind tunnel *(left center)* at Moffett Field looks like an ancient gramophone. It is here that the NASA Research Center tests its latest aeronautical designs. The dirigible hangars *(upper right)*, built for the Navy's long-vanished giant airships, are so huge that it's been known to rain in their vast interiors.

This windowless building is Lockheed's super-secret Blue Cube in Sunnyvale. It controls our military satellites in space. In the background is the Onizuka Air Force Base, named after Ellison Onizuka, the first Japanese-American astronaut, who died in the Challenger disaster.

(opposite) Just north of Moffett Field stands the white, twin-peaked Shoreline Amphitheater, scene of rock-and-roll and country western concerts all summer long. The Shoreline Golf Course lies between it and the Bay.

Look what El Niño did to these homes perched on a cliff's edge in Pacifica. Their residents were evacuated as their backyards fell into the sea, and the houses were later demolished.

(*opposite*) That tiny marker atop the pointed rock at the lower right designates the spot just south of the San Francisco border where the dread San Andreas Fault emerges from the sea to attack the Peninsula.

Take me above the ball game. . . It's opening day on April 7, 1998. The stadium, officially named "3-Com Park" in return for a large donation from that corporation, is still "Candlestick Park" to most San Franciscans. The battle over the name change will be moot when a new stadium opens in the city's downtown area in 2000. It will be called "Pac Bell Park."

(*opposite*) Pristine San Mateo with its tree-lined streets is the shopping center of the Peninsula.

SILICON VALLEY   Apple Computer

Long after World War II, Silicon Valley remained a bucolic preserve of orchards and
pasture land. But with the dawn of the technological age, it seems that every week
another new firm has opened its laboratory doors and another young multi-millionaire
has retired. Here are a few of the world's biggest players in this exciting new era.

(opposite) Oracle

Sun Microsystems

(opposite) The Netscape Communications Corporation

IBM

IBM Almaden Research

IBM Almaden Research

Silicon Graphics

(opposite) Advanced Micro Devices

Cisco Systems

Intel Corporation

(*opposite*) Downtown San Jose rises from a web of freeways. This formerly insignificant neighbor has now surpassed San Francisco in population and is determined to rival it in arts, culture and sports.

Occasionally there are holes in the summer fog that clings to the coast. Here's a glimpse of the sand and surf down near Portola Valley.

(*opposite*) Old-timers have it that during Prohibition in the 1930s smugglers used these caves south of Pacifica to hide liquor they had brought down from Canada.

THE EAST BAY

Gertrude Stein said there is no there there. Herb Caen, the ultimate San Franciscan, claimed you needed a visa to visit the place. The place is Oakland, which, from the air, looks like a thriving metropolis. That's lovely Lake Merrit in the center and the Oakland Estuary in the upper right.

(opposite) All Hail, Blue and Gold! The Berkeley campus of the University of California, famed for student riots, mediocre football teams and Nobel laureates. The Campanile, poking up in the center, points to Memorial Stadium just behind it.

The tower and grounds of Oakland's Mormon Temple. Inside is a branch of the world's largest genealogical research library in Salt Lake City. Those seeking their ancestors can search among the two billion names on file free of charge.

(opposite) The Hotel Claremont, a posh resort in the Berkeley hills that overcame an alcohol problem. Built in l915, the hotel survived Prohibition only to be told on Repeal that it was within one mile of the University of California campus and therefore couldn't serve liquor. In 1936 a female U.C student determined that the distance was actually one mile and a few feet. This heroine, who remains anonymous, was rightly awarded free drinks for life.

Verdant Tilden Park crowns the East Bay Hills. No fairways are steeper than on this golf course, and Lake Anza's sandy beach is just the spot for sun bathers and swimmers.

(opposite) Elephants and tigers! Killer whales and dolphins! Twenty-four – count 'em – thrilling rides! Marine World boasts that it's the "only combination wildlife park, oceanarium and theme park" on the planet. That exciting brew attracts more than a million visitors a year.

This is the Oakland Mole in 1925, where passenger trains from the East terminated. The last few miles of a traveler's journey to San Francisco were by ferry boat, and there was no more stirring way to arrive.

(opposite) Nowadays the Oakland Mole reaches out into the bay and is a thriving cargo port. Train passengers from the East now make the last few miles to San Francisco across the Bay Bridge on a bus with neither wind nor salt spray in their hair.

The serried streets of Berkeley lead up to the University of California, its campanile and its stadium. Beyond the Berkeley hills rises Mt. Diablo, at 3,849 feet the highest point in the Bay Area.

(opposite) Here's a surprise: Within the city of Oakland lies the Claremont Country Club, one of California's oldest (1894). A plaque on the first tee under the venerable Tudor clubhouse commemorates Sam Snead's first professional victory in the 1937 "Oakland Open." Its 18 rolling fairways border on the Mountain View and St. Mary's Cemeteries, which some of the older members consider a convenient location.

Looking over the small town of Benicia in the foreground to the busy city of Vallejo. The grassy area *(center)* is a 350-acre green belt purchased by the two communities to serve as a buffer zone between the old and the quaint and the new and the bustling.

(opposite) Suisun Bay spreads across the Delta where the mighty Sacramento and San Joaquin Rivers meet to flow to the ocean. This is the Grizzly Island Wildlife Area adjacent to Cordelia Slough, a resting place for thousands of waterfowl on their annual migrations.

THE NORTH BAY

Looking over Fort Baker to the Marin headlands where cars are being swallowed by the cottony fog that on summer afternoons so often smothers the Golden Gate Bridge.

(opposite) Looking west over Stinson Beach and the marshlands of the Bolinas Lagoon. Those little dots on the horizon beyond the Bolinas headlands are the Farallon Islands, the rookery of thousands of gulls and other birds.

Here's the San Rafael Rock Quarry on the Marin shore of the Bay. Men and machines have been mining a hard rock known as "gray wacke" here for close to a century. It's used in rip rap and as an aggregate in construction. The lovely lake at the bottom is actually a reservoir for use in the extraction process.

(opposite) From the air, the grim cell blocks of San Quentin look positively inviting. Built in 1852, the prison now houses some 6,000 inmates, many of whom can be seen in their orange uniforms taking the air in the exercise yards. The famed gas chamber, where 198 of the condemned have met their deaths, is on the ground floor of one of the small buildings that form the prison's easterly walls *(right center)*.

The afternoon fog attacks little Sausalito, just north of the Golden Gate. Settled by Portuguese fishermen, it was taken over after World War II by liberals and environmentalists who are now fighting politically with developers. The liberals' battle cry is, "Keep Sausalito funky," which it certainly is.

(opposite) These wooded hills overlooking the Golden Gate were long part of Ft. Barry, whose cannons were primed to defend the city from invading armadas. The cannons were never fired in anger.

119

The Sears Point Raceway lies at the north end of San Pablo Bay on the road to the wine country. Some 650,000 spectators pass through the gates annually to watch race cars and motorcycles whip around the winding two-and-a-half mile track.

(*opposite*) Looking over Tiburon, Belvedere, Richardson Bay and Sausalito to the ocean in the distance. The man-made Belvedere Lagoon (*center*) is the site of expensive homes and regattas for small sailboats. The inappropriately named San Francisco Yacht Club is on the Bay to its left.

Muir Woods with its giant redwoods is one of the area's major tourist attractions. From the air, one can see that its forests are remarkably lush and dense.

(opposite) The jaws of the Marin headlands just west of the Golden Gate reach out to clutch any unwary ship.

Blue water fills the green valleys of southern Marin. The entire area is either a state park or a preserved watershed and thus will remain a Mecca for hikers and environmentalists for generations yet to come.

Seadrift is an exclusive gated community built on a sandspit at the western end of Stinson Beach. It lies between the sea and the huge Bolinas Labgoon, home to sea lions, heron and other wildlife. Its houses surround its own man-made lagoon for swimmers and boaters. You can still buy a vacant beachfront lot for $1 million or so.

(opposite) The lovely Meadow Club lies in a lake-filled valley beneath Mt.Tamalpais. The virgin forests surrounding the golf course are owned by the Marin Municipal Water District and are thus preserved from developers.

127

Here's a family feud that's produced some fine wine. Opposite is the original Sebastiani Winery founded in the city of Sonoma in 1904 by Samuele Sebastiani. In recent years, the two grandsons who ran the firm, Don and Sam Sebastiani, had a falling out, and in 1991 Sam and his wife, Vicki, opened the Viansa Winery and Italian Market Place *(left)* on a hilltop outside of town. San Francisco Helicopter Tours now flies wine lovers to Viansa for tastings and a picnic lunch.

The beautifully landscaped Ferrari-Carano Winery founded by Don and Rhonda Carano in 1981 lies in the Dry Creek Valley just south of Lake Sonoma. The Italianate Villa Fiore houses the hospitality center and tasting room.

(opposite) This French chateau nestled in the Alexander Valley is the Jordan Winery. The chateau with its luxurious furnishings and guest rooms was built in 1972 to fulfill the visions of Tom Jordan, a successful Denver oil man. From its 275 acres of vineyards, the winery produces prize-winning Chardonnay and Cabernet Sauvignon.

Nestled in a curve of the River Road west of Santa Rosa are the white roofs of the Korbel Champagne Cellars. Three Korbel brothers created the winery in the 1870s and many of the buildings hark back to their native Bohemia. Owned today by the Heck family, the winery offers tours of its 100-year-old cellars and its Korbel History Museum, as well as a multimedia presentation on the production of sparkling wines.

The small, fastidious Sonoma-Coutrer winery produces only estate-bottled Chardonnay. The grapes are hand-picked from the winery's own vine-yards, hand sorted, barrel-fermented and aged in French oak. The winery's owner, Brice Coutrer Jones, is a cro-quet enthusiast, and the World Cro-quet Championship is held here every spring.

(opposite) This little jewel is the Quary-hill Botanical Gardens in the heart of the Sonoma Valley. This private enclave is dedicated to the conser-vation and preservation of endan-gered Asian species.

(opposite) Chateau Souverain selects its grapes from throughout Sonoma County to suit its varietals: The Alexander Valley for Cabernet Sauvignon, Merlot and Sauvignon Blanc; The Dry Creek Valley for Zinfandel; and the cooler climate of Caneros and The Russian River Valley for its Chardonnay and Pinot Noir.

For more then half a century, the Gallo label was thought of by most to indicate a cheap jug wine produced by Ernest and Julio Gallo in their huge Central Valley operation. But here is Gallo of Sonoma, where Ernest's grandchildren, Matt and Gina Gallo, are now turning out prize-winning Cabernets and Chardonnays. "Gallo of Sonoma is not your grandfather's Gallo," says a company spokesman.

The lovely community of Sonoma surrounds the historic Plaza in the center. It was in the Plaza that the Bear Flag was raised on June 14, 1846, to celebrate independence from Mexico and the creation of the California Republic. The Republic's Bear Flag flew just 26 days before the Stars and Stripes were hoisted.

THE NAPA VALLEY

Four thousand years ago, give or take, the Indians settled in this valley and called it Napa, meaning "plenty." Today, the valley offers plenty of wine, plenty of sunshine, plenty of good food and a vast plenty of euphoria.

The white monastic buildings of Sterling Vineyards just south of Calistoga look down on the long expanse of the Napa Valley. For visitors, it is reachable only by a tram that rises from the parking lot. The rewards are the spectacular view, a tasting room, a gallery of local artists and an illustrated tour of the wine making process.

The Culinary Institute of America, known happily in the valley as "The CIA," is housed in this sprawling chateau, once the home of the Christian Brothers Winery. In addition to its student body of professional chefs, the CIA offers a restaurant where their work can be tested by the general public.

(opposite) Charles Krug boasts of being the first winery built in the Napa Valley. It was founded in 1861 by a Prussian immigrant of that name. For the past half century the winery has been owned by the Mondavi family. Grandsons Peter and Marc Mondavi are now in charge.

Silverado Country Club and Resort offers eight swimming pools, twenty-three tennis courts and two golf courses to occupy your leisure time. The stately French-Italianate mansion, which now serves as the clubhouse, was built in the early 1870s by General John Franklin Miller, a Civil War veteran, and smacks of the ante-bellum South.

(opposite) In 1979 Champagne Mumm et Cie and Joseph E. Seagram & Sons brought sparkling wines to the valley by the *methode champenoise*, the proper designation of any champagne-like wine produced outside the Champagne district of France. To anyone unfamiliar with vintners' ethics, however, Mumm's is simply a fine champagne.

Sutter Home is the largest winery in the Napa Valley and dates back to 1874. Since 1947 it has been owned by the Trinchero family. More than 800 varieties of plants and herbs flourish in its extensive gardens, and, for overnight visitors, there's even a bed and breakfast in a Victorian house on the property.

(*opposite*) Niebaum-Coppola is the old Inglenook Winery, founded by Gustave Niebaum, a Finnish sea captain in 1887. Francis Ford Coppola, who makes not only films but wine, purchased it in 1978. The lovely Inglenook Chateau is the red-roofed building in the center, screened by trees and facing on its plaza.

Robert Mondavi is usually heralded as the Uncrowned King of the Napa Valley. He crushed his first grapes in 1966, and this is the winery from which he rules today. He and his wife, Margrit, stage jazz and classical music festivals in the summer. Traffic on Highway 29 in the foreground is often bumper-to-bumper on pleasant weekends.

(opposite) With Americans sipping more wines each passing year, vineyards have spread across the floor of the Napa Valley and now creep up the hillsides, producing these swirling abstract patterns.

Far Niente Winery is a name that evokes the spirit of the valley. It's from the Italian phrase, "Dolce far niente" — "How sweet it is to do nothing." It was hardly in that spirit, however, that the present owner, Gil Nickel, took over the abandoned, century-old stone winery in 1979, restored it and began producing some of the valley's finest chardonnays and cabernet sauvignons.

(opposite) The Clos Pegase Winery boasts prize-winning architecture that has starred in international exhibits. The clean, monumental lines are designed to evoke the earliest wine-making civilizations, such as Egypt, Crete and Mycenae. They encase a plethora of paintings, sculptures, reliefs and, yes, even a tasting room.

Beaulieu Vineyard is an old-time family winery, and look how it's grown. "BV," as it's better known these days, was founded in 1900 by Georges de Latour. His name on a label followed by "Private Reserve" commands a high price today. BV wines now grace many a dinner table.

(opposite) Peter Newton terraced 560 acres of steep Spring Mountain above St. Helena to create the vineyard that bears his name. Earlier in his career, the veteran wine maker founded, and later sold, the famous Sterling Vineyards.

Calistoga Mineral Water got off to a spectacular start in 1920 when Giuseppe Musante decided to drill a well to supply his candy store and soda fountain. Instead of underground water, he hit a geothermal pocket. The resulting geyser knocked Musante off his ladder, shot 250 feet into the air and flooded half of downtown Calistoga. Today, the mineral water plant is one of the largest in the United States.

(opposite) The Sattui family has been pressing St. Helena grapes ever since great-grandfather Vittorio Sattui came over from Italy in 1882. In addition to a tasting room the small stone winery provides visitors with a gourmet deli and tree-shaded picnic grounds.

No Mickey Mouse operation, the Silverado Winery, established by the Walt Disney family in the 1970s, produces 80,000 cases a year of Merlot, Cabernet, Chardonnay and other fine wines under the supervision of his granddaughter, Diane Disney Miller, and her husband, Ron. Perched atop a knoll, the tasting room attracts visitors with a fine arts gallery and a bucolic view of the Napa valley.

(opposite) Just a stone's throw from their Silverado Winery is the Walt Disney family home, where his widow, Lillian, lived for 20 years before her death in 1997 at the age of 98. It was she who created the famed lily pond, one of the most delightful spots in the Napa Valley. The home is now used as a family retreat.

The Beringers have been making wine in the Napa Valley since 1876. The family home, a 17-room mansion called the Rhine House *(center)* was modeled on the Beringers' ancestral estate in Germany and now owns a listing in the National Register of Historic Places. Behind the house are "coolie-built" caves dug more than a hundred years ago to store the casks of aging wine.

(opposite) Here's a noble landmark, Opus One, owned jointly by the Baroness Philippine de Rothschild and Robert Mondavi, often described as the king of the Napa Valley. And if that's not noble enough, the prices of the wine range upward from $60 a bottle. Crowning a knoll on the valley floor, the winery is the site of seminars, tastings, tours, art exhibits and summer jazz concerts.

Here's a rare sight: machine pickers crawling through vineyards near Yountville. Once hailed for their efficiency, economy and their ability to pick grapes at night, machines now have been abandoned by most growers in favor of hand pickers. It was found that the machines, by straddling the rows and shaking off the grapes, did too much damage to the vines.

(opposite) Beyond vineyards and oak-studded hills lies Lake Berryessa. The 25-mile long lake was created in 1957 by the Monticello Dam which flooded the lovely Berryessa Valley over the protests of environmentalists and to the delight of thousands of fishermen and boaters.

The sun sets over Seal Rocks where hundreds of sea lions (not seals) have wintered from the beginning of time. Most now prefer the more comfortable floating docks at Pier 39.

(opposite) A cottony blanket of fog arrives for the cocktail hour in the cool, gray city of love.

(back cover) A single light glows faintly from Alcatraz as the
setting sun enflames the sky behind the Marin hills.